My GOVERNMENT

Standing in the President's Shoes

Sarah Machajewski

Cavendish
Square

New York

Published in 2016 by Cavendish Square Publishing, LLC
243 5th Avenue, Suite 136, New York, NY 10016

Website: cavendishsq.com

This publication represents the opinions and views of the author based on his or her personal experience, knowledge, and research. The information in this book serves as a general guide only. The author and publisher have used their best efforts in preparing this book and disclaim liability rising directly or indirectly from the use and application of this book.

CPSIA Compliance Information: Batch #WS15CSQ

All websites were available and accurate when this book was sent to press.

Library of Congress Cataloging-in-Publication Data

Machajewski, Sarah.
Standing in the president's shoes / by Sarah Machajewski.
p. cm. — (My government)
Includes index.
ISBN 978-1-50260-461-3 (hardcover) ISBN 978-1-50260-460-6 (paperback)
ISBN 978-1-50260-462-0 (ebook)
1. Presidents — United States — Juvenile literature. 2. United States — Politics and government — Juvenile literature.
I. Machajewski, Sarah. II. Title.
JK517.M28 2015
352.230973—d23

Editorial Director: David McNamara
Editor: Amy Hayes
Copy Editor: Cynthia Roby
Art Director: Jeffrey Talbot
Designer: Alan Sliwinski
Senior Production Manager: Jennifer Ryder-Talbot
Production Editor: Renni Johnson
Photo Research: J8 Media

The photographs in this book are used by permission and through the courtesy of: Cristina Ciochina/Shutterstock.com, cover; Pete Souza/File:Barack Obama greets Kavya Shivashankar the 2009 Scripps Spelling Bee Winner.jpg/Wikimedia Commons, 4; Look and Learn/Bridgeman Art Library, 6; Diana Walker/Time Life Pictures/Getty Images, 8; Brendan Smialowski/AFP/Getty Images, 9; Sean Gallup/Getty Images, 10; Ron Sachs-Pool/Getty Images, 12; Library of Congress, 14; Olivier Douliery-Pool/Getty Images, 16; Alex Wong/Getty Images, 18; Kevork Djansezian/Getty Images, 20; Joe Raedle/Getty Images, 21; Ralph Crane/The LIFE Picture Collection/Getty Images, 22; Bill O'Leary/The Washington Post/Getty Images, 24; Toby Talbot/AP Images, 26; Jupiterimages/Creatas/Thinkstock, 27; Martin H. Simon-Pool/Getty Images, 28.

Printed in the United States of America

TABLE OF CONTENTS

Kavya Shivashankar, the 2009 Scripps Spelling Bee winner, meets President Obama in the White House.

A government is an institution that **determines** how a country, state, or city is run. It makes laws and also makes sure these laws are carried out. A government's decisions greatly affect our lives. If you've ever visited a public park or mailed a letter, you've used something provided by your government. Who is in charge of these important functions? It's the men and women who have been **elected** or appointed as our **representatives**. The president holds the most important job in government. Let's take a look at the president's job by spending a day in his shoes!

After taking the oath of office, George Washington kissed the Bible that was used to swear him in.

CHAPTER ONE

Meet the President

The presidency is one of the oldest jobs in government. The position was created in 1787 at meetings now known as the Constitutional Convention. Two years later, George Washington was elected as the first president of the United States. The job has stayed much the same since then.

What have presidents been doing for the last 125 years? The president is the head of the executive branch of our country's federal government. This branch makes sure laws are carried out. The president is also the head of his or her **political party**.

Members of Congress look on as former president Bill Clinton signs a bill into law.

The president plays a key role in the lawmaking process by approving or rejecting laws created by Congress. The president reads **bills** written by members of the House and the Senate. If the president agrees with the bill, he or she signs it and it becomes a law. If the president does not agree with the bill, it gets rejected. This is called a veto. Signing a bill is an important **responsibility**. It means that any law that exists does so because the president agreed that it should. It also means that the president can keep some laws from passing.

The president has a lot of power over our country's laws. That power, however, is limited in some cases. For instance, presidents cannot write bills themselves. Someone in Congress must do it.

Part of the president's job is delivering speeches before the United States Congress.

President Barack Obama meets with the chancellor of Germany, Angela Merkel.

Lawmaking is just one part of the president's job. The Constitution of the United States lists all the president's responsibilities. It says the president is the commander-in-chief of the US military and the chief executive of the federal government. That means he or she has the power to carry out laws and make **treaties** with other countries. It's also the president's job to create federal policies, oversee the national **budget**, and appoint people to government positions. To pardon, or forgive, criminals is also an important responsibility. The president can call a meeting of Congress and can also dismiss it. Finally, he or she must receive important visitors to the White House.

The president holds the top position in the US government and has a lot of responsibilities. The president can hire and fire people, and has to manage any questions or issues that come up with employees. It's the president's job to make sure the right people are in the right role, and that they're doing a good job. This way our government can run successfully.

The president also represents the United States to other countries. Some of these countries are friendly with the United States while others are not. Still, the president must keep all US **citizens** happy and safe. This may seem as if the entire country is resting on the president's shoulders. Would you like having this kind of job?

Serving the Nation

The president serves the entire country. That means the president answers to over three hundred million people!

President Barack Obama waves to the crowd during his inauguration, or the ceremony that marks the beginning of the presidential term.

CHAPTER TWO

A Day with the President

Presidents must stick to a schedule in order to get everything done. A typical day could include meetings, phone calls, and public appearances— all before breakfast! All the presidents have **organized** their days a little differently. Let's take a look at a typical day for the US president.

MORNING

Some presidents get up early enough to exercise before work. President Barack Obama has said that a typical day for him starts with working out. Former president

Even presidents must eat breakfast!

Franklin D. Roosevelt even had a pool installed in the White House so he could swim.

Next is breakfast, which the president may have with family. If a president is very busy, he or she eats breakfast while looking over notes or the schedule for the day.

The first official task on the president's agenda is usually around 10:00 a.m. The president and vice president

Getting to Work

Throughout history, presidents have arrived at work at different times. John F. Kennedy began work at 7:30 a.m., while Chester Arthur was known for not starting until at least 10:00 a.m.

meet with staff in the Oval Office for the Presidential Daily Briefing. They review **intelligence** and important news.

AFTERNOON

A president's day is filled with appointments. Running the country is a big task, and the president often needs assistance. The White House staff helps. Each White House staffer is in charge of a certain job. They report their progress to the president, who helps them choose how to handle something, or asks them to change what they're doing.

The president's afternoon also includes meetings with officials from state governments and or leaders from other countries. Sometimes these meetings take

A Working Lunch

Sometimes the president works during lunch and often invites special groups of people, such as teachers or African-American leaders, to have lunch at the White House. It's a chance to hear these groups' concerns.

Part of a president's day may be spent helping others. Serving food to people in need is one way to help.

place at the White House, but the president can take the presidential limo to meetings that happen elsewhere. The president may also hold press conferences on important issues. And that's all in just one afternoon!

EVENING

The president usually wraps up meetings around 5:00 p.m. However, the work isn't over. Important dinners, press conferences or interviews, and **fundraising** events can make up the president's evening schedule.

It may seem as if the president's job is never done. However, many presidents have made sure to spend time with their families. President Obama has dinner with his family every night at 6:30 p.m. He has said this is important because he's still a dad, even though he's the president!

After dinner, the president may catch up on e-mails or review the schedule for the next day. Then, it's lights out until the work starts all over again.

CONCLUSION

Being the president isn't easy. The president is on call twenty-four hours a day, seven days a week. The day is busy from the first beep of the alarm clock until bedtime. The president may even have to work during the night. If you were the president, how would you plan your day?

Presidential Hobbies

Some presidents have had hobbies that help them relax. Franklin Roosevelt had a large stamp collection. Dwight Eisenhower had a putting green put in at the White House for golf. The White House even has a bowling alley!

The road to the presidency is long, but moments such as the inaugural ceremony make it worth the effort.

CHAPTER THREE

Becoming the President

There are three **requirements** a person must meet in order to become president. A **candidate** must be at least thirty-five years old, a US citizen, and must have lived in the United States for at least fourteen years. Meeting these requirements is the easiest part of becoming president!

A person may want to be president if they have ideas about how our government should work. They may think they can make our country stronger, safer, or more successful. The first step for many future presidents is to become active within their political party. By being active, their name will then become familiar to the public.

People who want to become president must tell the public how their ideas will help the country.

Campaigning is the most important part of becoming president. Campaigning is when candidates try to show voters that they are the best person for the job. They may **participate** in community events. They may hold rallies—meetings of large numbers of people—and give speeches. They want to appear smart and well spoken, and show voters how their ideas could work.

The next step is a caucus. During the caucus, candidates from the same political party debate each other. This means they ask and answer questions about each other's ideas. Then, the parties hold a primary. A primary is when party members vote for the candidate who could best represent them in a national election. Winners have a good chance at becoming that party's presidential candidate.

After the caucus there is the national convention, or gathering. Each political party holds a convention where they choose their presidential candidate. The presidential candidates then announce whom they've chosen as their vice presidential candidates. The president and the vice president are the only two positions in the United States that are elected by the entire country.

Hilary Clinton hoped to win these voters' support during the 2008 campaign season.

National Conventions are very exciting events.

The two presidential candidates then campaign for the general election. They travel the country and give speeches. They meet with Americans and try to earn their support. As the election gets closer, the candidates debate each other on television.

The presidential election happens every four years in November. The American people vote on Election Day. When Americans vote, they may think they're voting for the president. They're actually voting for electors. Electors are people who have promised to support the same candidate as the voters. The electors belong to a group called the Electoral College, and it directly elects the president.

This is how the Electoral College works: if a citizen votes for the democratic presidential candidate, he or she is actually voting for his or her state's democratic electors. If more people in that state vote for one candidate more than another, that presidential candidate wins all of that state's electoral votes.

States have different numbers of electoral votes based on how much representation they have in Congress. A potential president wants to win states that have the most electoral votes, because the candidate with the most electoral votes wins.

At the end of Election Day, the country finds out who will be the new president! He or she is inaugurated, or sworn-in, in January.

How Many Terms?

A president's term is four years long. The Constitution limits the president to two terms, though it didn't always used to be this way. President Franklin D. Roosevelt actually served four times in office!

Meeting with students is an important—and fun—part of the president's job.

CHAPTER FOUR

A Future in Politics

Do you think you'd like to be president one day? Get started now! The best way to prepare for a life in politics is to get involved with your government. You can start by learning how your local government works.

Every county, town, and city has a local government. It handles lawmaking, running the local police and fire departments, maintaining parks, and more. Local governments serve the people who live there, with a goal of making residents happy. If you have an idea for how your town could be better, speak up and make your

Kids like you are the future of government. It's important to make your voice heard.

voice heard! You can attend town hall meetings or write letters to local officials. Sharing your ideas can help change your community for the better. It's similar to how the president shares ideas to help make the whole country better.

Another way to get involved is to volunteer, or spend time doing something to help others. You can help with events that are happening around your town. Start a canned-food drive, or get a group of people together to clean up parks or a local beach. Many presidents get their start by actively working in their communities.

The most important way to prepare for a life in politics is to know the concerns of people around you. Attending meetings and watching the news are great ways to learn about issues. By educating yourself on what's happening, you can help make changes. If you ever have the chance to meet an elected official, ask questions. You may ask what they're doing to keep the citizens happy, or what ideas they have to fix a

Do you have ideas about how you can help your community? Speak up and take action!

problem. You may face these same questions when you're president one day!

It's not easy to become the president. It takes years of hard work. Many candidates begin their careers as lawyers and congressmen. They have to know and care about issues. They have to prove they would be a good leader. Finally, they have to get the American people to support them. History's best presidents have **adapted** to changing issues. More importantly, they make changes based on what the people want. If you ever become president, the issues you handle may be different than

Volunteering is a good way to prepare for a life in politics.

those today's president is facing. If you start getting involved now, the future of our government could be that much brighter—especially when a very prepared person steps into the role!

Get Involved!

- Write a Letter to the President
  http://www.whitehouse.gov/contact/write-or-call
- Young Democrats of America
  http://www.yda.org
- Young Republican National Federation
  http://yrnf.com/#sthash.ZX1k4071.dpbs

adapt To change.

bill A proposed or projected law; bills are set before Congress.

budget A plan for how money should be spent.

candidate A person who runs in an election.

citizen A person who belongs to a country.

determine To cause something to happen in a certain way.

elect To choose someone to hold a public office.

fundraise To raise money.

intelligence Military or political information.

organize To order activities in a certain way.

participate To take part in.

political party A group of people who share the same political ideas.

GLOSSARY

representative Someone who is chosen to speak for others.

requirement A condition that needs to be met before something can happen.

responsibility Something that a person is required to do as part of their job.

treaty A formal agreement.

FIND OUT MORE!

BOOKS

Davis, Todd, and Marc Frey. *The New Big Book of U.S. Presidents: Fascinating Facts about Every President, Including an American History Timeline.* Philadelphia, PA: Running Press Books, 2013.

Hajeski, Nancy J. *The Big Book of Presidents: From George Washington to Barack Obama.* New York: Sky Pony Press, 2015.

Richmond, Benjamin. *What Are the Three Branches of the Government? And Other Questions about the U.S. Constitution. Good Question.* New York: Sterling Children's Books, 2015.

WEBSITES

Kids.gov: A Safe Place to Learn and Play
http://kids.usa.gov

PBS – "PBS KIDS: The Democracy Project"
pbskids.org/democracy

Scholastic – "Scholastic News: You're the President"
http://teacher.scholastic.com/scholasticnews/games_quizzes/electiongame/game.asp

MEET THE AUTHOR

Sarah Machajewski is the author of several children's books on subjects ranging from science to social studies, and everything in between. She enjoys researching current events and keeping track of today's changing political landscape. Machajewski graduated from the University of Pittsburgh in 2010 and lives in Buffalo, New York.